QUESTIONS
& ANSWERS

ABOUT

The United Methodist Church

THOMAS S. McANALLY

QUESTIONS & ANSWERS

ABOUT

The United Methodist Church

QUESTIONS AND ANSWERS ABOUT THE UNITED METHODIST CHURCH

Editor: Rachel B. Hagewood
Designer: Ed Maksimowicz

Web addresses were correct and operational at the time of publication.

Print
ISBN: 9781501871139
PACP10538754-01
ePub
ISBN: 9781501871146
PACP10538755-01

18 19 20 21 22 23 24 25 26 27 — 10 9 8 7 6 5 4 3 2 1

MANUFACTURED IN THE UNITED STATES OF AMERICA

QUESTIONS & ANSWERS

ABOUT

The United Methodist Church

INTRODUCTION

In the popular off-Broadway play, *Sister Mary Ignatius Explains It All for You*, a nun answers questions about the faith on flash cards, presumably from the audience. She routinely flips through the cards, answering questions in a very matter-of-fact manner, but stops abruptly when she comes to the question, "If God is all-powerful, why does he allow evil in the world?" With a furtive glance to the left and right, she quickly moves to the next card!

We're not trying to "explain it all for you" or to provide exhaustive, scholarly answers or encyclopedic definitions. The questions included in this book are those often asked by church members and others interested in The United Methodist Church. They have been grouped into categories only in an attempt to provide organization to this resource; the questions mostly stand alone. The assumption is that if a question is asked frequently by others, you may also have asked it—or wished you had. I have attempted to answer these questions with as much simplicity as possible. Admittedly, the answers are incomplete.

If you want more detailed information, a list of recommended resources is included at the close of this booklet. Also, you may wish to talk to your pastor or peruse the denomination's official website, www.umc.org.

TABLE OF CONTENTS

SACRAMENTS

What is required of me to be a United Methodist?
Baptism ushers you into the Christian church universal, the family of Christ. When baptized you will be asked to

- renounce the spiritual forces of wickedness, reject the evil powers of the world, and repent of your sin;
- accept the freedom and power God gives you to resist evil, injustice, and oppression; and
- confess Jesus Christ as your Savior, put your whole trust in his grace, and promise to serve him as your Lord, in union with the church which Christ has opened to people of all ages, nations, and races (The Baptismal Covenant I, *The United Methodist Hymnal* [UMH]).

Your pastor may require that you participate in a membership class before being baptized or taking church membership vows.

After baptism, then what?
To be received into United Methodist membership, you will be asked "to be loyal to Christ through The United Methodist Church and do all in your power to strengthen its ministries." Last, you will be received as a member of a particular congregation by committing yourself to faithfully participate in its ministries by your prayers, your presence, your gifts, your service, and your witness. Baptism isn't the end of the process; it's just the beginning of a lifelong journey of faith that is lived out in community with your local church.

What does the church teach about baptism?
"Through the Sacrament of Baptism we are initiated into Christ's holy church. We are incorporated into God's mighty acts of salvation, and given new birth through water and the Spirit. All this is God's gift, offered to us without price" (The Baptismal Covenant II, UMH).

If I have already been baptized in another Christian denomination, must I be rebaptized to be a United Methodist?
No, your previous baptism is accepted.

Are there any exceptions?

Yes. One example, found in *The Book of Resolutions of The United Methodist Church, 2016*, recommends that converts from The Church of Jesus Christ of Latter-day Saints be offered the sacrament of Christian baptism following a period of intensive exploration and instruction in the Christian faith because that church, according to *The Book of Resolutions of The United Methodist Church, 2016*, "presents itself as a faith tradition outside the parameters of historic, apostolic Christianity."

What if I want to be baptized a second time?

Baptism is an act of God, and God does it right the first time. Our side of the covenant relationship with God will need recommitment and reaffirmation, but God always remains faithful on the divine side. Talk to your pastor about using a meaningful service for remembering and renewing your earlier baptism vows.

How is baptism done in The United Methodist Church?

Sprinkling is most commonly used, but pouring and immersion are also permissible. United Methodists are more concerned with the symbolism and meaning of the event than the exact form that might have been used in early times.

United Methodists baptize babies. Is it necessary for salvation?

Regardless of age, the sacrament of baptism is initiation into the household of faith, the means by which a person is "incorporated by the Holy Spirit into God's new creation" (The Baptismal Covenant II, UMH). When an infant is baptized, the parents promise to raise the child in a Christian home, and the congregation recognizes its responsibility in the Christian nurture of the child. Baptismal vows are usually reaffirmed by the child at confirmation. Baptism is not absolutely necessary for salvation. An infant who dies without having been baptized is as much within the love and care of God as the baptized infant.

What is the difference between baptism and confirmation?

The *sacrament* of baptism for a person of any age acknowledges God's unconditional love and claim on the recipient and should not be repeated. The *rite* of confirmation is a person's response to God. Confirmation is most often observed in local churches when youth, baptized as infants, make their own public declaration of faith. However, people of any age may choose to reaffirm their baptismal vows in a public worship service more than once.

What sacraments are observed by United Methodists?

Two: Baptism, a non-repeatable initiation into the body of Christ, and the Lord's Supper, a regularly repeatable celebration of Communion of the body of Christ. Other events such as confirmation, marriage, and funeral services are obviously significant and important, but they are not considered sacraments. A sacrament is a ceremony considered especially sacred because God is acting through it or because it is a sign or symbol of a significant reality. The denomination's Articles of Religion call the sacraments "certain signs of grace, and God's good will toward us."

What is the difference between Communion and the Lord's Supper?

Holy Communion, the Lord's Supper, and the Eucharist all refer to the sacrament celebrated by United Methodists, but each term highlights a different aspect of this act of worship: *communion* with God and with one another, a *holy meal* to which we are invited by Jesus, and *thanks* to God for gifts of creation and salvation. The sacrament is a celebration and remembrance of God's grace and mercy in Jesus, of the resurrection of Christ, and of Christ's continuing presence with us.

In the Communion service, what is meant by the "body and blood of Christ"?

The bread and wine represent the body and blood of Jesus as he spoke of them at the Last Supper with his disciples. We do not believe that the elements literally turn into the body and blood of Christ, but we do believe that Jesus Christ is truly present in Holy Communion. The divine presence is a living reality and can be experienced by participants. It is not only a remembrance of the Last Supper and Crucifixion, but also a celebration of Christ's presence.

How often do United Methodists observe Holy Communion?
Most congregations observe Holy Communion at least once a month, usually on the first Sunday, and on special days of the Christian year. Some congregations offer Communion weekly. There is a move toward more frequent celebrations to recover practices of the early church and early Methodism. John Wesley, Methodism's founder, instructed believers to celebrate Holy Communion "as often as [one] can."

Why does the church use grape juice instead of wine in Holy Communion?
Although the historic and ecumenical Christian practice has been to use wine, the use of unfermented grape juice by The United Methodist Church and its predecessors since the late nineteenth century expresses pastoral concern for recovering alcoholics, enables the participation of children and youth, and supports the church's witness of abstinence from alcoholic beverages. The term *wine* continues to be used because of its biblical and historical antecedents, even when unfermented grape juice is used.

Are children permitted to participate in the Lord's Supper?
Yes. The Lord's Supper is open to all people. Children, members of the covenant community, may not fully comprehend what is going on, but they know when they are excluded.

Is anybody excluded from participating in the Lord's Supper?
Anyone may participate who responds affirmatively to the invitation: "Christ our Lord invites to his table all who love him, who earnestly repent of their sin and seek to live in peace with one another" (A Service of Word and Table I, UMH). United Methodists practice "open Communion," meaning the Lord's Table is open to all who re-

spond to Christ's love, regardless of age or church affiliation. People who have not been baptized may respond in faith to the invitation and receive Communion, but the church is encouraged to counsel these persons and nurture them toward baptism.

Can Holy Communion be celebrated at my wedding?

Yes, but the invitation should be extended to everyone present. It is not appropriate for only the couple or family to commune.

Who is authorized to administer the sacraments of baptism and Holy Communion?

Ordained elders. Others, including licensed pastors, commissioned elders, and deacons, may be given authority to administer the sacraments but only in a particular congregation or charge to which they are appointed.

Can we take the Communion elements consecrated by our pastor and receive them several days later at our youth retreat?

No. Consecrating elements ahead of time is inappropriate. The bread and wine are to be consecrated and consumed in the presence of the gathered community of faith. The Table is extended when lay members take the consecrated elements immediately after the service to members confined at home, in a nursing home, or in a hospital.

A friend from another denomination half-jokingly says one can be a United Methodist and believe anything. Why does that impression exist among some people?

United Methodists recognize the right of Christians to differ in doctrine, requiring only the essential beliefs that God is our Creator, that Jesus the Christ is our Lord and Savior, and that the Holy Spirit is ever present with us. While we acknowledge the primacy of Scripture in theological reflection, our attempts to grasp its meaning always involve the tradition of the church, personal experience, and the ability to reason for ourselves. The United Methodist Church is not a creedal church that requires members to subscribe to a closely detailed system of beliefs. This does not mean, however, that United Methodists are not committed to basic Christian doctrines. Both the Articles of Religion and the Confession of Faith are embodied in our *Book of Discipline* as the doctrinal standards of the church. In addition, the *Standard Sermons* and *Notes Upon the New Testament* from Methodism's founder, John Wesley, are included in the existing and established standards of doctrine and are accepted as landmark documents for United Methodists. We affirm core Christian doctrines, such as the Trinity—Father, Son, and Holy Spirit—both in personal experience and in the community of believers; salvation by grace through faith in Christ as Savior; the universal church; the reign of God as both a present and future reality; the authority of Scripture in matters of faith; and the essential oneness of the church in Jesus Christ. "Our Theological Task," a twelve-page section of *The Book of Discipline*, encourages all United Methodists to reflect on God's gracious action in their lives.

You say the church is not creedal, but I often hear creeds recited at United Methodist worship services. Why?

While we have not made rigid acceptance of a creed the basis for uniting with the church's fellowship, we do not hesitate to use creeds in worship. They allow us to recall and affirm ancient and modern attempts to articulate the Christian tradition from a variety of perspectives.

Why does the creed I often hear in worship affirm belief in the catholic church?

The "holy catholic church," a phrase from The Apostles' Creed, indicates our belief that the church is essentially one, universal, and open to all. It is not a specific reference to the Roman Catholic Church.

Are pastors told what Scriptures to use in their sermons?

No, United Methodist pastors have total freedom to select their own Scriptures. However, many use an ecumenical guide known as *The Revised Common Lectionary*. This three-year cycle of biblical texts usually includes lessons from the Old Testament, an Epistle, and one of the Gospels. Frequently, they include a selection from the Psalms as well. If the lectionary is followed, a congregation will hear the major biblical themes over a three-year period and will explore some texts that otherwise might be neglected. Many congregations appreciate knowing that the same biblical texts are being heard and explored with Christians around the world on the same day.

Why are the colors changed on our altar, and the stoles worn by our pastor and choir members?

The United Methodist Church and many other Christian bodies use color to mark important events in the life of the church. *The United Methodist Book of Worship* encourages "creativity with colors and signs for days and seasons," but most of our churches use the following colors: purple or blue (Advent); white (Christmas, Easter, All Saints' Day, Christ the King); purple (Lent, sometimes with black being used on Ash Wednesday and Good Friday); red (Pentecost); and green at other times (Ordinary Time).

What is different or distinctive about being a United Methodist?

No Christian doctrines are exclusively United Methodist. However, we have distinctive emphases including

- the availability of God's grace for all;
- the essential unity of faith and works;
- salvation as personal and social;

- the church as a community of Christ's disciples who seek to share in God's mission;
- the inseparability of knowledge (intellect) and vital piety (devotion to religious duties and practices) as components of faith;
- seeking holiness of heart and life both as individuals and in society;
- a cooperative ministry and mission in the world; and
- the link between Christian doctrine and Christian living.

How do United Methodists view other Christian bodies?

We strive for Christian unity and cooperation. Our constitution affirms our ecumenical commitment: "As part of the church universal, The United Methodist Church believes that the Lord of the church is calling Christians everywhere to strive toward unity; and therefore it will pray, seek, and work for unity at all levels of church life." This ecumenical spirit exists at every level of United Methodism, including councils or associations of churches and cooperative mission and ministries in local communities and locations around the globe.

HISTORY AND DEMOGRAPHICS

How old is The United Methodist Church?

Methodism's roots are in eighteenth-century England. American Methodism formally organized in 1784 with the creation of The Methodist Episcopal Church. Following divisions, unions, and reunions, the present United Methodist Church was created in 1968 with the merger of The Methodist Church and The Evangelical United Brethren Church. The Evangelical United Brethren Church was the result of a 1946 union of the Church of the United Brethren in Christ and The Evangelical Church. The Methodist Church was the result of a 1939 union of The Methodist Episcopal Church, The Methodist Protestant Church, and The Methodist Episcopal Church, South.

Where did the church get its name?

John and Charles Wesley and a few other young men attending Oxford University met regularly in 1729 for intellectual and spiritual improvement and to help one another become better Christians. So systematic were their habits of religious duty and their rules of conduct that other students mockingly referred to them as *Methodists*. *United* in our name comes from The Evangelical United Brethren Church, which united with The Methodist Church in 1968 to form The United Methodist Church.

John Wesley

But aren't there other Methodist denominations?

Yes, many, but not all have Wesleyan or Methodist denominations in their name. The World Methodist Council, organized in 1881, is an association of eighty Methodist, Wesleyan, and uniting churches representing 80.5 million people in 133 countries. The uniting churches are those in which Methodists have joined with others to form a new denomination, such as The United Church of Canada.

Charles Wesley

How many US denominations have roots in the Wesleyan movement?

There are at least fourteen denominations in the US with Wesleyan roots. The largest of these, with seven million members, is The United Methodist Church. It ranks second in US Protestant Church membership, after the Southern Baptists, but is more geographically widespread with at least one congregation in most counties and almost as many churches as there are US post offices. Other US denominations with Wesleyan roots that are members of The World Methodist Council include The African Methodist Episcopal, Christian Methodist Episcopal, African Methodist Episcopal Zion, Church of the Nazarene, Free Methodist Church, and The Wesleyan Church.

What is the largest Wesleyan denomination outside the United States?

Among autonomous Methodist denominations worldwide, The Korean Methodist Church leads with 1.4 million members, 6,721 churches, and 11,674 clergy. The largest congregation in the worldwide Wesleyan family, with 45,212 members, is Kumnan Methodist Church in Seoul, Korea.

How big is The United Methodist Church?

US membership is now about 7 million; membership outside the United States has grown to 5.6 million.

How much has United Methodist membership declined?

Combined church membership peaked at eleven million in the two predecessor denominations of The United Methodist Church (Methodist and Evangelical United Brethren) in 1965. There has been steady decline since that time in the United States, but there has been growth in other countries. Much of this growth has been recorded in the Philippines and parts of Africa. All new membership is declining, particularly professions of faith, but new membership is holding steady as the leading way we gain new members (as compared to transfers from other denominations). Average attendance at the principal weekly worship service has declined by more than one million persons since 1968.

What's the largest congregation in the denomination?

Of the seven United Methodist congregations in the United States reporting more than 10,000 members each, five are in Texas and three of those are in Houston. Windsor Village in Houston is the largest with more than 18,000 members, followed by Highland Park, Dallas, with nearly 17,000 members. Church of the Resurrection in

Leawood, KS, has nearly 15,000 members; White's Chapel in Fort Worth, TX, has nearly 14,000; Glide Memorial in San Francisco, CA, has more than 13,000; The Woodlands in Houston, TX, has more than 12,000; and Saint Johns in Houston, TX, has more than 10,000.

More than 70% of United Methodist churches in the United States have fewer than 200 members, representing 25.5% of the denomination's total membership, 30.5% of worship attendance, and 39.5% of Christian formation group attendance (Sunday school, small groups, and so forth). While the majority of our churches are considered small membership churches (under 200 members), the majority of our members (74.3%) attend congregations with more than 200 members.

When did African Americans become part of Methodism?
African Americans have been part of the Methodist movement from the earliest days of American Methodism. At the organizing Christmas Conference of 1784 in Baltimore, persons in attendance included

Harry Hosier

ed Richard Allen and Harry Hosier, both popular black preachers and former slaves. Anne Sweitzer, a slave, was on the roll of the first Methodist society in America, founded in Maryland in 1764. A servant named Bettye helped start the John Street Church in New York, the first formal meetinghouse in America. Two other black women contributed money to help build that chapel. Thousands of black Methodist converts, both slave and free, were worshipping alongside white converts in camp meetings and revivals.

Isn't there an African Methodist denomination in the United States?
There are several historically African American Methodist denominations. The three largest, with a combined membership of more than 4.5 million, are:
- The African Methodist Episcopal Church, formally organized in 1816. It traces its origin to an incident at St. George's Meth-

odist Episcopal Church in Philadelphia in 1787 when a group of African Americans left the church to protest racial discrimination.

- The African Methodist Episcopal Zion Church, which dates from 1796 when it was organized by a group of members protesting discrimination in the John Street Methodist Church in New York City.
- The Christian Methodist Episcopal Church, which was established in 1870 after an agreement between white and black members of The Methodist Episcopal Church, South.

How ethnically diverse is The United Methodist Church in the United States?

Of the 7 million US members, less than ten percent are ethnic minority: 427,000 African American; 92,373 Asian American; 76,864 Hispanic American; and 21,208 Native American. Of the church's 46 active US bishops, ten are African American (six male, four female), five are Asian American (all male), three are Hispanic American (one male, two female), and 28 are Caucasian (seventeen male, ten female). There are 5.6 million members outside the United States.

Are women well represented among leaders in The United Methodist Church?

Women make up 58 percent of total United Methodist membership in the United States. Of the church's 66 active bishops, 17 are women. About 135 of the 423 US district superintendents are women. Of 45,210 ordained US clergy, about 12,300 are women. While women clergy have increased in number in recent decades, there are still relatively few women in senior pastor positions of large churches. The most recent survey indicated that about half of seminary students preparing for ministry in United Methodist seminaries in the United States were women.

ORGANIZATION

How is The United Methodist Church organized?

The denomination is a democratic and representative organization. The manner by which the church is organized, the selection of leaders, and the way it uses its resources are determined by a majority of voting members at local, regional, and international meetings called "conferences."

Do laypeople have much to say about what happens in the church?

In the early days of American Methodism, clergy made most decisions for the church. Today, laity and clergy have equal voice in annual, jurisdictional, and general conferences. There are also guidelines that encourage fair representation of women, young adults, and youth in decision-making. Of course, at the local level, laypersons are deeply involved in every aspect of the church's mission and ministry.

Where is the headquarters of The United Methodist Church?

There is no one headquarters and no single spokesperson or authority, such as a pope or archbishop. The only body that can speak for The United Methodist Church is General Conference, which meets every four years at a different location around the country, traditionally rotating among the five US jurisdictions.

Churchwide agencies are established by General Conference to support and administer the work of the church. These boards and agencies are located in various cities, including Atlanta, GA; Nashville, TN; Washington, D.C.; and New York. You can find a list of the general agencies and their respective Web addresses at the end of this booklet.

What happens to the money I put in the offering plate?

In the United States, about 85 cents of every dollar given in the offering plate stays in the local church; 7 cents goes to work at the district, annual conference, and jurisdictional level; 6 cents goes for benevolent giving; and 2 cents goes to general apportionments. Your church's expense figures will vary, depending on your support of annual conference benevolences.

The money that United Methodists give to the broader United Methodist Church through apportionments allows the church, as a worldwide connection, to do more than any one church or even regional connection of churches is able to do alone. We support mission, ministry, education, disaster relief, and other essential needs throughout the globe. The cost of our Christ-centered global ministry is significant, but it is only a small portion of the local church budget.

What is a charge conference?

A "charge" is usually one local church, but sometimes two or more smaller churches are connected together to make up one charge. The charge conference—composed of all members of the church council or leadership body—meets at least once a year to oversee and direct the ministry of the church, to set salaries for the pastor and other staff, and to elect members for organizational bodies within the church including the church council. The district superintendent usually presides. The charge conference is the link that connects the local church to the annual conference and the larger church. A "church conference," at which all church members participate and vote, may be authorized by the district superintendent.

What is a district superintendent?

A district superintendent (often referred to as a "D.S.") is an ordained elder appointed by a bishop to supervise a region (or district) of about fifty churches. These districts vary greatly in geographic area. An individual is not appointed pastor and district superintendent simultaneously. District superintendents are appointed for a year at a time, just like pastors.

What is an annual conference?

The term is a bit confusing because the title refers both to regional units and to the meetings held by those units each year. There are 56 annual (regional) conferences in the United States, supervised by 46 bishops. There are 75 annual conferences in Africa, Europe, and the Philippines, supervised by 20 bishops. (Some annual conferences are grouped into episcopal areas, where one bishop presides over multiple annual conferences.) Each year an equal number of lay members from local churches and the ordained clergy gather for annual conference sessions to approve, among other things, programs and budget, and to speak to social concerns. Every four years these bodies elect delegates to jurisdictional and general conferences.

What is a jurisdictional conference?

A jurisdictional conference is a meeting held every four years in each of five geographic jurisdictions in the United States primarily to elect and assign bishops, determine the boundaries for episcopal areas, and implement General Conference legislation. Each US jurisdiction includes eight to fifteen annual conferences.

What is a central conference?

In Africa, Europe, and the Philippines, there are a total of seven geographical regions called central conferences, each of which is comprised of annual conferences and divided into several episcopal areas.

What is General Conference?

The only entity that can speak officially for The United Methodist Church, General Conference meets every four years in locations that rotate among the five jurisdictions in the US. Special sessions at other times may be called by the Council of Bishops. The international body includes no more than 1,000 delegates: half clergy, half laity. General Conference votes on legislation and resolutions that make up the church's organizing documents. Updated versions of these documents, *The Book of Discipline* and *The Book of Resolutions*, are produced after each General Conference.

How are General Conference delegates elected?

Every four years, members of each annual conference elect delegates to General Conference. The number of clergy and lay delegates to which an annual conference is entitled is computed on two factors: the number of clergy members of the annual conference and the number of members of local churches in the annual conference. Clergy vote for clergy; laypersons vote for laypersons.

The names of colleges and universities such as Southern Methodist University and Nebraska Wesleyan suggest they are related to The United Methodist Church. What is the relationship, if any?

One of the first actions taken by American Methodists when they organized in 1784 was to create Cokesbury College in Abingdon, Maryland. Since that time, The United Methodist Church and its predecessor denominations have been affiliated in some way with 1,200 educational institutions. Today, there are 119 United Methodist-related schools, colleges, and universities, including 13 schools of theology and 12 historically black colleges and universities. These institutions have widely varying relationships to the denomination. Some schools receive major financial assistance from a unit of the church or the entire denomination, while others receive little or no direct financial aid. One example of a university that receives denomination-wide support is Africa University, located in Zimbabwe. Launched by the denomination in 1972, it has more than 5,000 graduates.

What about hospitals and retirement homes?

As with schools, colleges, and universities, their relationship to the church varies. The health and welfare ministries related to The United Methodist Church serve more than 32 million people in 1,555 locations across the United States and provide more than $2 billion in charity care annually. These include 152 older adult ministries; 105 community service ministries; 63 children, youth, and family service ministries; and 52 hospitals and health care systems.

What is a bishop?

A bishop is an ordained elder, elected by a jurisdictional or central conference, to serve in the top office of the church. US bishops are elected for life. They are considered general superintendents of the entire church, but are assigned to four-year terms to oversee the work of the church in a particular area. The normal tenure in one area is eight years; the limit is twelve. Mandatory retirement age for a bishop is 68, although a few may continue until age 72, depending on the time they reach the age of 68. Rules vary in central conferences where some bishops are elected for four-year terms. Currently, the church has 66 active and 101 retired bishops. All are members of the Council of Bishops, but only active bishops may vote in that body.

How are bishops paid?

All US bishops receive the same salary amount, according to a formula determined by the General Conference. In addition to salary, each bishop is provided an episcopal residence owned by the annual conference or conferences within the episcopal area. Bishops in central conferences outside the United States are paid according to the pay scales in the economies of their respective regions.

How does my church get a pastor?

All ordained members (elders and deacons) of an annual conference are appointed annually by the bishop, whether they serve as pastors of congregations or in extension ministries outside the local church. Appointments of pastors is a consultative process involving the appropriate local church committee, the district superintendent, and the bishop. The bishop has final authority in appointment-making.

Why is my pastor moved?

Methodism has a long tradition of *itinerant* clergy. As Methodism began in America, pastors served circuits, traveling around a specified region and ministering to Methodist communities within the area. Today, all ordained elders of the annual conference are subject to annual appointment by a bishop and must be willing to go where sent. This itineracy assures every pastor a church and every church a pastor. It also matches the gifts and graces of an individual with the needs of a particular church or area of service, and provides a broader foundation of ministries developed by a variety of leadership styles brought by each individual pastor over time. Ordained deacons do not itinerate. They are appointed by the bishop, but typically find their own place of appointment.

How long does a pastor stay in one church?

A pastor is appointed for one year at a time, but most stay at an appointment for multiple years. The average tenure is about four years.

How are pastors paid?

Local churches determine the amount of the pastor's salary. Each annual conference sets a minimum salary, which it subsidizes if the local congregation cannot pay it in full.

Are clergy ever fired?

Ordained elders may voluntarily "locate"—choose to step outside the regular itinerant or appointive system—or may be forcibly removed by "involuntary location." Ministerial credentials may be taken from a clergyperson if he or she is found guilty of charges spelled out in the church's *Book of Discipline*. Sometimes credentials are voluntarily surrendered.

We have deacons and elders on the staff of my congregation. What's the difference?

Deacons and elders are both ordained, but the focus of their ministry is somewhat different. Both deacons and elders are ordained for ministries of word and service. Deacons are set apart for ministries of compassion and justice, elders for ministries of sacrament and order. Both are appointed by bishops. Most elders are appointed as church pastors or institutional chaplains. Deacons lead God's people in compassion and justice ministries in the world and may lead faith-formation opportunities. They may be appointed to serve primarily in congregations or primarily in settings outside the local church.

What do I call my pastor?

Pastors often invite adult members of their congregation to call them by their first name. Otherwise, *Pastor* before their first or last name is appropriate. The use of *Reverend* as a title of respect is commonly used, but debatable. Some dictionaries list the word as a noun: "a member of the clergy." The most widely used stylebook for journalists says *Reverend*, when used before an individual's name, should be preceded by the word *the* because, unlike the case of *Mr.* or *Mrs.*, the abbreviation does not stand for a noun. Some argue that *the Reverend* should not be used because it is an indirect reference, just as *the Honorable* is for a judge. Pastors with doctoral degrees sometimes prefer that *Dr.* be used before their last names. Clergy appointed to ministries beyond the local church may prefer titles more descriptive of their day-to-day work: *Chaplain, President, Dean, Professor,* and so forth. So, when in doubt, ask your pastor what he or she would like to be called!

How can I become an ordained minister?

First, talk with your pastor or another clergy person about your interest or sense of God's call to full-time ministry. Your pastor can guide you through a process that begins with an application for candidacy. You must have been active in The United Methodist Church or a United Methodist Church member for a minimum of one year and be approved by your local church, a district committee, and a conference board of ordained ministry. Normally, you must complete a bachelor's degree and three years of study at an approved school of theology. The United Methodist Church also licenses local pastors who complete a non-degree course of study and serve a congregation or extension ministry performing the duties of a pastor for the duration of their appointment. They are not guaranteed an appointment, and their license is no longer valid once the appointment ends.

How long have United Methodists had women clergy?

Women were ordained in some predecessor denominations of The United Methodist Church in the late 1800s, but were not given equal rights with their male colleagues until 1956 in The Methodist Church. Today, ordained women elders are members of their annual conferences and as such are fully eligible for appointment as pastors, district superintendents, special appointments beyond the local church, and election as bishops. Female deacons are eligible for any appointment suitable to the ministry of a deacon. Women are not officially denied positions of leadership anywhere in the church because of gender.

How many ordained women are serving the church today?

The most recent statistics indicate that of the 45,210 clergy in the United States, 12,300 are women. Our best records show approximately 34% of district superintendents are women. Of the 46 active bishops in the US, sixteen are women. Of the twenty active bishops outside the US, one is a woman. While the number of women clergy has increased in recent decades, there are still relatively few women in senior pastor positions of large congregations.

Why didn't our newly appointed pastor join our church with her husband and children?

United Methodist clergy are members of their annual conference, the body to which they are amenable in the performance of their duties. Since their membership is with the annual conference, they do not become members of the local churches they serve.

What are the major challenges facing The United Methodist Church today?

Ask a dozen people, and you may get a dozen different answers: secularization, US membership decline, lack of denominational loyalty, competition for time, and the growing number of *nones* who profess no religious convictions or affiliations. Some church leaders contend we have an identity crisis and must renew our focus on theology—who God is, what God is doing, and what we are to be and do in response. Other leaders warn that the church's future witness depends on attracting more young and diverse people.

But is one issue most critical?

Unquestionably, the most divisive issue facing the church at this time is homosexuality, a topic that has been debated by delegates at every quadrennial General Conference since 1972. Debate was so contentious at the most recent 2016 General Conference in Portland, OR, that delegates halted discussion and asked the bishops for help leading the church to a long-lasting resolution. The bishops proposed to create a representative group to explore the church's options and make a proposal to the Council of Bishops. The 32-member "Commission on a Way Forward" will make its final report to the Council of Bishops in May 2018. With that report in hand, the bishops will formulate their own recommendations for consideration by delegates to a special-called session of the General Conference in St. Louis, MO, on February 23–26, 2019.

What is the church's official stance on homosexuality?

United Methodists around the globe represent a broad spectrum of beliefs, opinions, and convictions about LGBTQ people. Hammered out by delegates at the past twelve General Conferences, the official stance of The United Methodist Church

- acknowledges that all people are children of God and of sacred worth;
- implores families and churches not to reject or condemn lesbian and gay members and friends;

- supports "basic human rights and civil liberties" due all persons, regardless of sexual orientation;
- supports efforts to stop violence and other forms of coercion against all persons, regardless of sexual orientation;
- describes the "practice of homosexuality" as "incompatible with Christian teaching";
- bans "self-avowed practicing homosexuals" from being ordained or appointed as pastors;
- forbids pastors from performing, and churches from hosting, gay marriage ceremonies;
- prohibits churchwide funds from being used to "promote the acceptance of homosexuality," but does not limit the church's ministry in response to the HIV epidemic;
- affirms sexual relations only in "monogamous, heterosexual marriage" and supports laws that define marriage as between one man and one woman; and
- affirms the right of all people, regardless of sexual orientation or gender identity, to be free from bullying and "unwanted aggressive behavior."

How are positions on social matters determined by the church?

Only the General Conference, a global body of no more than 1,000 delegates—half clergy and half lay—speaks officially for the church. A set of social principles is produced by the delegates at each conference as a "prayerful and thoughtful effort . . . to speak to the human issues in the contemporary world from a sound biblical and theological foundation." These principles are a "call to all members to a prayerful and studied dialogue of faith and practice." Obviously, United Methodists do not agree on all these principles. Most are intended to be "instructive and persuasive," not church law. Official resources of the church, such as church school curriculum, must reflect the official positions of the church.

What is the church's stand on abortion?

The church affirms the sanctity of unborn human life, but recognizes "tragic conflicts of life with life that may justify abortion." The church says decisions concerning abortion should be made only after thoughtful and prayerful consideration by the parties involved, with medical, family, pastoral, and other appropriate counsel. Late-term abortion is opposed except when the physical life of the mother is in danger. Abortion is rejected as a means of birth control or as a means of gender selection. Ministries that seek to reduce unintended pregnancies are encouraged.

What is the church's stand on divorce?
The church recognizes divorce as regrettable, but endorses the right of divorced persons to remarry.

What is the church's stand on the death penalty?
The church opposes the death penalty (capital punishment) and urges its elimination from all criminal codes.

What is the church's stand on gun control?
United Methodist congregations are encouraged to support laws that reduce gun violence, including universal background checks on all gun purchases and banning "large-capacity ammunition magazines and weapons designed to fire multiple rounds each time the trigger is pulled."

What if I want to change a position of the church with which I disagree?
Each United Methodist has a right to petition General Conference. Your pastor can assist you. Every petition is considered, although similar petitions are usually grouped together. You may also contact delegates from your annual conference to the General Conference. Normally, these individuals are elected at annual conference sessions in the year preceding the General Conference.

Where can I find official positions and rules of The United Methodist Church?
Two books will be most helpful: *The Book of Discipline* and *The Book of Resolutions*. Both are produced every four years following General Conference sessions. *The Book of Discipline* is our manual of procedures and regulations. It covers every phase of church life: doctrine;

guidance for Christian behavior; procedure and ritual for becoming a church member or a minister; details for organizing and administering local churches, districts, and conferences, as well as churchwide boards and agencies; and rules of church law. *The Book of Resolutions* includes statements on social concerns approved by General Conference delegates.

How can I get answers to questions not in this book?

Talk to your pastor, check out the recommended resources, or visit the denomination's official website: www.umc.org.

A key resource for additional information is *The United Methodist Church Handbook—Therefore, Go: Making Disciples of Jesus Christ for the Transformation of the World,* United Methodist Communications, 2017. This resource is available in four languages online at: http://www.umcgiving.org/resource-articles/united-methodist-handbook-languages.

You can also find a list of general agencies of The United Methodist Church and their websites listed at the end of recommended resources.

RECOMMENDED RESOURCES

Anderson, E. Byron. *The Meaning of Holy Communion in The United Methodist Church*. Nashville: Discipleship Resources, 2014.

The Book of Discipline of The United Methodist Church, 2016. Nashville: The United Methodist Publishing House, 2016.

The Book of Resolutions of The United Methodist Church, 2016. Nashville: The United Methodist Publishing House, 2016.

"By Water and the Spirit: A United Methodist Understanding of Baptism." *The Book of Resolutions of The United Methodist Church*. Nashville: The United Methodist Publishing House, 2016.

Crain, Margaret Ann. *The United Methodist Deacon: Ordained to Word, Service, Compassion, and Justice*. Nashville: Abingdon Press, 2014.

Frank, Thomas Edward. *Polity, Practice, and the Mission of The United Methodist Church*. Nashville: Abingdon Press, 2006.

Jones, Scott J. and Arthur D. Jones. *Ask: Faith Questions in a Skeptical Age*. Nashville: Abingdon Press, 2015.

Joyner Jr., F. Belton. *United Methodist Questions, United Methodist Answers: Exploring Christian Faith*. Revised edition 2015. Louisville, KY: Westminster John Knox Press.

Stamm, Mark W. *Our Membership Vows in The United Methodist Church*. Nashville: Discipleship Resources, 2014.

Stamm, Mark W. *The Meaning of Baptism in The United Methodist Church*. Nashville: Discipleship Resources, 2016.

Stamm, Mark W. *Sacraments & Discipleship, Understanding Baptism and the Lord's Supper in a Methodist Context*. Nashville: Discipleship Resources, 2003.

Stamm, Mark W. *Extending the Table, A Guide for a Ministry of Home Communion Serving*. Nashville: Discipleship Resources, 2009.

"This Holy Mystery: A United Methodist Understanding of Holy Communion." *The Book of Resolutions of The United Methodist Church*. Nashville: The United Methodist Publishing House, 2016.

The United Methodist Hymnal. Nashville: The United Methodist Publishing House, 1989.

The United Methodist Book of Worship. Nashville: The United Methodist Publishing House, 1992.

Tuell, Jack M. *The Organization of The United Methodist Church*. 2009–2012 Edition. Nashville: Abingdon Press, 2010.

Willimon, William H. *This We Believe: The Core of Wesleyan Faith and Practice*. Nashville: Abingdon Press, 2010.

Yrigoyen Jr., Charles. *Belief Matters: United Methodism's Doctrinal Standards*. Nashville: Abingdon Press, 2001.

General Agencies of The United Methodist Church

Discipleship Ministries: www.umdiscipleship.org
General Board of Church & Society: www.umcjustice.org
General Board of Global Ministries: www.umcmission.org
General Board of Higher Education & Ministry: www.gbhem.org
General Commission on Archives & History: www.gcah.org
General Commission on Religion & Race: www.gcorr.org
General Commission on the Status and Role of Women: www.gcsrw.org
General Commission on United Methodist Men: www.gcumm.org
General Council on Finance & Administration: www.gcfa.org
The Connectional Table: www.umc.org/connectionaltable
The United Methodist Publishing House: www.umph.org
United Methodist Communications: www.umcom.org
United Methodist Women: www.unitedmethodistwomen.org
Wespath (formerly General Board of Pension and Health Benefits): www.wespath.org